# LE CORDON BLEU
## HOME COLLECTION
# · CHOCOLATE ·

PERIPLUS

# contents

*recipe ratings*  ❀ *easy*  ❀ ❀ *a little more care needed*  ❀ ❀ ❀ *more care needed*

# Flourless chocolate cake

*Served with Chantilly cream and a sprinkling of flaked almonds, this dense chocolate cake makes a lovely dessert, but is perfect for a little chocolate indulgence on any occasion.*

*Preparation time* **30 minutes**
*Total cooking time* **50 minutes**
**Serves 8**

**3/4 cup lightly packed soft light brown sugar**
**I cup unsalted butter, softened**
**4 eggs, separated**
**6 oz. semisweet dark chocolate,**
  **coarsely grated**
**I 1/4 cups ground almonds**
**3 tablespoons sugar**
**2 1/2 tablespoons sliced almonds**

**CHANTILLY CREAM**
**I 1/4 cups whipping cream**
**few drops of vanilla extract**
**2 tablespoons confectioners' sugar**

1  Lightly grease a 9-inch round cake pan and line the bottom with waxed paper. Preheat the oven to 300°F.
2  Cream the brown sugar and butter together in a large bowl until light and pale. Beat in the egg yolks one at a time, beating well after each addition. Stir in the chocolate and ground almonds until well combined. In a separate bowl, beat the egg whites until stiff, beat in the sugar, then fold it carefully into the chocolate mixture in four additions. Do not overfold, or the mixture will lose its volume. When there are no more streaks of white in the chocolate mixture, pour into the pan and bake for 50 minutes, or until it springs back when lightly touched in the center. Cool the cake completely before removing it from the pan.
3  To make the Chantilly cream, beat the cream with the vanilla and sugar in a large bowl until it is standing in stiff peaks. Keep chilled until needed.
4  To serve, cut the cake into wedges and serve with the Chantilly cream alongside and a sprinkling of the sliced almonds.

*Chef's tips* This cake can be baked in a square pan for an alternative presentation to wedges.

For extra speed, you can grate the chocolate quickly by using the grater attachment of a food processor.

# Chocolate profiteroles

*The name profiterole is derived from the French word* profit, *and originally meant a small gift, which is just what these chocolate-smothered cream puffs are.*

Preparation time **30 minutes**
Total cooking time **30 minutes**
**Serves 6**

**PROFITEROLES**
**1 teaspoon sugar**
**generous pinch of salt**
**1/3 cup unsalted butter**
**1 cup bread flour or all-purpose flour, sifted**
**4 eggs, lightly beaten**
**1 egg, lightly beaten and strained, to glaze**

**FILLING**
**1 1/2 cups whipping cream**
**1 1/2 tablespoons sugar**
**1–2 drops vanilla extract**

**confectioners' sugar, to dust**
**Chocolate sauce, to serve (see page 60 for the recipe)**

1  To make the profiteroles, preheat the oven to 400°F. Brush a baking sheet with melted butter and refrigerate until needed. Put 1 cup water with the sugar, salt and butter in a deep saucepan, bring to a boil and remove from the heat. Immediately add all the flour to the liquid and stir with a wooden spoon. Return the pan to low heat and cook, stirring constantly, until the mixture rolls off the sides of the pan. Remove from the heat and allow to cool until lukewarm. (If it is too hot the eggs will cook when they are added.) Gradually add the eggs, a little at a time, beating well between each addition. The mixture loosen with each addition, but thickens with beating. Stop adding the eggs once the mixture drops freely from the spoon. Spoon into a pastry bag fitted with a 3/8-inch plain nozzle.

2  With the nozzle about 1/2 inch above the baking sheet, pipe well-spaced balls 1 inch in diameter, then stop the pressure on the bag and quickly pull away. Brush the top of each ball with the strained egg, making sure that it does not run down the sides as it will burn during cooking. Lightly press down the top of each ball with the back of a fork to ensure an even shape when rising. Bake for 15–20 minutes, or until well risen and golden brown. The profiteroles should sound hollow when the base is tapped. Make a small hole in the base of each profiterole using the point of a small knife. Transfer to a wire rack to cool thoroughly.

3  To make the filling, beat the cream, sugar and vanilla together until stiff peaks form. Spoon the cream into a pastry bag fitted with a small round nozzle and pipe into the base of each profiterole.

4  To serve, stack the profiteroles in a pyramid in a glass bowl or on individual plates. Dust lightly with sifted confectioners' sugar and serve with the warm chocolate sauce drizzled over.

# White chocolate crème brûlée

*Hidden beneath this dessert's crackly sugar topping lies a creamy, white chocolate custard. The two textures combine beautifully to create this delicious variation of the traditional crème brûlée.*

*Preparation time **10 minutes + refrigeration***
*Total cooking time **25 minutes***
***Serves 6***

**1 1/2 cups heavy cream**
**1 vanilla bean**
**4 oz. white chocolate, chopped**
**6 egg yolks**
**1/3 cup granulated sugar**

**1** Pour the cream into a medium saucepan. Split the vanilla bean lengthwise and scrape out the seeds using the tip of a small pointed knife. Add the seeds and the bean to the cream and heat slowly until just at boiling point, over low to medium heat, allowing the flavor to infuse. Remove from the heat.

**2** Put the chocolate in the top of a double boiler over hot water and allow to melt slowly, off the heat, stirring occasionally until smooth. Remove the insert from the water. Stir in the yolks until well combined, then stir in the hot cream.

**3** Place the insert back over the water over moderate heat and stir constantly with a wooden spoon until the mixture thickens and coats the back of a spoon. Strain the custard through a fine sieve, discarding the vanilla bean. Pour the mixture into six 3 x 1 1/2 inch, 1/2-cup soufflé dishes or custard cups and set aside to cool. Refrigerate for several hours or overnight, or until they are firmly set.

**4** Finish the crème brûlée by sprinkling with the granulated sugar and placing under a hot broiler until the sugar turns dark golden brown. Do not add the topping more than 2 hours before serving. Serve chilled.

***Chef's tips*** Crème brûlée can be prepared in advance, to the end of step 3.

For an alternative topping to the traditional crème brûlée, divide 3 oz. of melted bittersweet chocolate evenly between the servings.

# Chocolate fondue

*Tradition states that if you drop your fruit into the fondue you must kiss the person opposite you.*

Preparation time **15 minutes**
Total cooking time **10 minutes**
**Serves 4**

**1 1/4 cups whipping cream**
**3 tablespoons milk**
**1 vanilla bean**
**1 lb. semisweet chocolate,**
   **finely chopped**
**1 banana**
**3 apples**
**4 slices fresh or canned pineapple**
**1/2 pint strawberries**

1 Place the cream and milk in the top of a double boiler. Split the vanilla bean lengthwise and scrape the seeds into the mixture. Place the boiler insert over direct heat and slowly heat until just at boiling point. Remove from the heat, discard the vanilla bean and stir in the chocolate until melted and smooth. Keep the fondue warm by placing the insert over lukewarm water.

2 Cut the fruit into large slices or chunks, depending on the type of fruit. Leave the strawberries whole.

3 To serve, skewer a mixture of fruits for each person and serve with a small dish of fondue on each individual plate. Alternatively, serve the fondue in the center of the table with the fruit and allow each person to dip one piece of fruit at a time into the fondue.

**Chef's tip** Vary your fruit selection to take advantage of each season.

# Chocolate terrine

*Even a small slice of this terrine is guaranteed to have you suffering from a chocolate overdose. The milk and dark chocolate mousse is surrounded with a layer of sponge cake, and topped with a rich chocolate coating.*

Preparation time **1 hour + refrigeration**
Total cooking time **15 minutes**
Serves **10–12**

### GENOISE SPONGE CAKE
**4 eggs**
**1/2 cup sugar**
**2/3 cup all-purpose flour**
**2 tablespoons unsweetened cocoa**

### MILK CHOCOLATE MOUSSE
**1 1/4 cups heavy cream**
**5 oz. milk chocolate, chopped**
**2 tablespoons sugar**
**2 egg yolks**

### SEMISWEET CHOCOLATE MOUSSE
**1 1/4 cups heavy cream**
**5 oz. semisweet chocolate, chopped**
**2 tablespoons sugar**
**2 egg yolks**

### CHOCOLATE GLAZE
**1 cup milk**
**10 oz. semisweet chocolate, chopped**
**1/4 cup sugar**

1  To make the génoise, preheat the oven to 400°F. Line two 12 x 7 x 11/2-inches jelly roll pans with waxed paper. Put the eggs and sugar in the top of a double boiler and place over a pan of barely steaming water. Beat with an electric mixer for 5–7 minutes, or until the mixture is thick and creamy, and has doubled in volume. The mixture should never be hot, only warm. Transfer the mixture to a mixing bowl and continue beating until cold. Sift the flour and cocoa together, and carefully fold into the egg mixture. Stop as soon as the flour and cocoa are just combined. Pour into the pans and bake on the middle rack of the oven for 5–6 minutes, or until springy and shrinking from the paper. Turn out onto a wire rack. Put another rack on top, turn over, remove the top rack and leave to cool, then peel away the paper. Trim the cakes and use them to line a 71/2 x 31/2 x 23/4 inch, 7-cup terrine or mold. Reserve a slice of cake 71/2 x 31/2 inches to fit on top of the terrine.

2  To make the milk chocolate mousse, whisk the cream in a large bowl until it leaves a trail as it falls from the whisk. Put the chocolate in the top of a double boiler over hot water, off the heat, making sure the insert is not touching the water. Leave the chocolate to melt slowly, then remove the insert from the water. Dissolve the sugar in 3 tablespoons water in a small saucepan over low heat and bring to a boil. Put the egg yolks in a small bowl and begin to beat them. Pour the bubbling syrup into the yolks and beat constantly until the mixture is thick and cold. Add to the chocolate and mix quickly to combine. Do not overmix. Add the whipped cream and carefully fold in with a plastic spatula or metal spoon.

3  To make the semisweet chocolate mousse, repeat step 2, replacing the chopped milk chocolate with the chopped semisweet chocolate.

4  Pour the milk chocolate mousse into the cake-lined mold, smooth the surface with the back of a spoon, then pour in the semisweet chocolate mousse. Cover with the reserved cake and freeze for 1 hour or refrigerate for 2 hours.

5  To make the glaze, heat the milk until just at boiling point. Add to the chocolate and mix well. Dissolve the sugar in 1/4 cup water and bring to a boil. Add to the chocolate. Remove the terrine from the freezer and turn onto a wire rack. Lay a plate under the rack and pour the glaze over the terrine. Transfer to a clean plate and serve at room temperature.

# Chocolate ice cream cups

*Ice cream dates back thousands of years where it began as a form of sorbet made of snow and honey. While this rich chocolate ice cream bears little resemblance to its humble ancestor, it is just as much of a delicacy. And, unlike the ancient sorbet, this ice cream can be enjoyed even when the snow isn't falling.*

*Preparation time **20 minutes + overnight freezing***
*Total cooking time **10 minutes***
*Serves 4–6*

**2 cups milk**
**1/2 vanilla bean, split lengthwise**
**3 oz. semisweet chocolate, chopped**
**4 egg yolks**
**1/3 cup sugar**

**CHOCOLATE CUPS**
**12 oz. semisweet chocolate, chopped**

**1** Heat the milk, vanilla bean and chopped chocolate in a saucepan, stirring until just at boiling point. Remove from the heat. Prepare a large bowl of iced water. Beat the egg yolks and sugar together until thick and pale. Pour in a third of the hot milk, blend and add this mixture to the pan with the rest of the milk. Cook over medium heat very slowly, stirring constantly, until the mixture thickens and coats the back of a spoon. When a finger is drawn across the coating, the line should not close over the spoon again. Do not allow to boil, or the eggs will overcook and the mixture will separate. Cool the mixture as quickly as possible by putting the pan straight into the bowl of iced water. Strain into a pitcher.
**2** Pour the mixture into an ice cream machine and churn for 15 minutes, or until set. The ice cream will be soft and may be served now or spooned into a 1-quart container and frozen until firm. If you do not have an ice cream machine, pour the strained mixture into a 1 quart container and freeze until just firm. Transfer to a large bowl and beat with an electric mixer until thick and pale. Return to the container, cover and freeze until firm. Beat once more before pouring back into the container and freezing overnight.
**3** To make the chocolate cups, follow the method in the Chef's techniques on page 63. When the cups are set, fill with scoops of the ice cream and serve. These ice cream cups are particularly delicious served with a fruit sauce or fresh fruit.

# Cinnamon and chocolate chip cookies

*If one of these sweet little morsels is delicious on its own, won't they be twice as delicious when two of them are sandwiched together with raspberry jam?*

*Preparation time **15 minutes + 20 minutes refrigeration***
*Total cooking time **10–15 minutes***
***Makes about 30***

**2 egg yolks**
**I teaspoon vanilla extract**
**2/3 cup unsalted butter, softened**
**3/4 cup confectioners' sugar**
**2 1/2 cups all-purpose flour**
**1/2 teaspoon baking powder**
**generous pinch of salt**
**1 1/2 teaspoons ground cinnamon**
**1/2 cup semisweet chocolate chips**
**1/2 cup raspberry jam**

**1** In a small bowl, lightly mix together the egg yolks, vanilla and 2 tablespoons water. In a large bowl, using an electric mixer or a wooden spoon, cream together the butter and confectioners' sugar until pale and light. Gradually add the yolk mixture.

**2** Sift together the flour, baking powder, salt and cinnamon, and add to the butter mixture. Stir until the flour is almost incorporated, then add the chocolate chips. Do not overwork the mixture. Using your hands, draw the mixture together into a rough ball of dough, wrap in plastic wrap and refrigerate for at least 20 minutes. Preheat the oven to 350°F.

**3** Roll the dough out on a lightly floured surface to a thickness of 1/4 inch. Cut out rounds with a 1 1/4-inch plain cutter, place on a baking sheet and bake for 10–15 minutes, or until light golden brown. Remove from the baking sheet and cool on a wire rack.

**4** Spread the base of one cookie with the raspberry jam and attach it to the base of another cookie to make a sandwich. Continue spreading with the raspberry jam until all the cookies are sandwiched together.

***Chef's tip*** The unfilled chocolate chip cookies will keep in an airtight container for up to a week. Once filled with the raspberry jam, their storage life is limited to 1 or 2 days.

# Chocolate brownies

*The aroma of a batch of brownies baking may be irresistible, but it doesn't compare with the sensation of sinking your teeth into the finished product. The thick chocolate frosting makes these twice as delectable.*

*Preparation time **20 minutes + refrigeration***
*Total cooking time **50 minutes***
***Makes about 16***

**3/4 cup unsalted butter, softened**
**I tablespoon vanilla extract**
**3/4 cup sugar**
**1/3 cup chopped semisweet chocolate**
**2 eggs, lightly beaten**
**3/4 cup all-purpose flour**
**pinch of salt**
**I teaspoon baking powder**
**I 1/2 cups walnuts, coarsely chopped**

**FROSTING**
**1/3 cup heavy cream**
**2/3 cup chopped semisweet chocolate**
**3 tablespoons unsalted butter, softened**

1  Grease an 8-inch square baking pan, and sprinkle with flour or line the bottom with waxed paper. Cream the butter, vanilla extract and sugar together in a large bowl with a wooden spoon or an electric mixer, until light and fluffy. Preheat the oven to 325°F.

2  Put the chocolate in the top of a double boiler over hot water, off the heat, making sure the insert is not touching the water. Leave the chocolate to melt slowly, stirring until smooth, then remove the insert from the water.

3  Gradually add the eggs to the creamed butter in about six additions, beating well after each addition, then stir in the melted chocolate.

4  Sift together the flour, salt and baking powder into a bowl, and add the chopped walnuts. Add to the chocolate mixture, and stir until just combined. Pour into the pan and bake for 45 minutes, or until firm and springy to the touch of a finger. Cool in the pan.

5  To make the frosting, pour the cream into a small saucepan and heat until just at boiling point. Remove from the heat and add the chocolate. Stir to melt, then whisk in the butter. Transfer to a bowl and refrigerate until cooled and slightly thickened before spreading on top of the brownies. Refrigerate until the frosting is just set. Cut the brownies into squares to serve.

***Chef's tips*** If you want you can use pecans instead of walnuts.

These chocolate brownies are superbly moist and will keep in an airtight container for up to a week.

# False truffles

*While the outside may deceive you into mistaking these for ordinary truffles, false truffles are far more wicked—balls of chocolate ice cream, smothered with rich chocolate ganache and rolled in cocoa.*

*Preparation time 30 minutes + 1 hour freezing*
*Total cooking time 5 minutes*
*Makes 12*

**1 cup best-quality chocolate ice cream**
**unsweetened cocoa, to dust**

**GANACHE**
**8 oz. semisweet chocolate, chopped**
**1 cup heavy cream**
**3 tablespoons sugar**

1 Line a baking sheet with waxed paper. Scoop 12 small balls from the ice cream using a melon baller or a teaspoon. Place on the baking sheet and freeze for at least 1 hour.
2 To make the ganache, put the chocolate in a bowl. Put the cream and sugar in a medium saucepan, and stir over low heat until the sugar has dissolved. Pour the cream mixture over the chocolate and leave it to melt for a few minutes, then gently stir until smooth. Keep stirring every 10 minutes for about 1 hour, or until cool.
3 Sift the cocoa into a shallow bowl. Once the balls of ice cream are frozen solid, remove a few at a time. Dip into the cooled ganache and immediately roll in the cocoa powder. Return the finished truffles to the freezer and repeat with the remaining balls.

*Chef's tips* Ganache—a superbly rich chocolate icing—must not be warm or it will melt the ice cream, nor must it be too cold or it will be too thick to coat the ice cream properly.
   Once they are frozen, the finished truffles may be kept in an airtight freezer bag for up to 1 month. Roll again in cocoa before serving, if necessary.

# Chocolate sorbet

*One scoop of this rich sorbet should be sufficient for most, but rarely is for true chocaholics.*

*Preparation time* **30 minutes + overnight freezing**
*Total cooking time* **5–10 minutes**
***Serves 6***

**3/4 cup sugar**
**1/2 cup unsweetened cocoa**
**4 oz. semisweet chocolate, chopped**

**RASPBERRY SAUCE**
**4 cups fresh raspberries**
**2 tablespoons confectioners' sugar**
**few drops of lemon juice**

1 Put 2 cups water with the sugar in a medium saucepan. Heat gently, stirring to dissolve the sugar, then bring to a boil. Remove the saucepan from the heat and add the cocoa and chocolate. Whisk to melt the chocolate and blend smoothly.

2 Return the saucepan to the heat and bring to a boil. As bubbles just break across the surface, immediately remove from the heat, place the saucepan in a bowl of iced water and leave for at least 10 minutes, or until thoroughly cooled. Pour the mixture into an ice cream machine and churn for 20 minutes, or until set. Pour into a 1-quart container and freeze overnight. If you don't have an ice cream machine, pour the mixture into a 1-quart container and freeze for 3 hours, or until firm. Scoop into a large bowl and beat with an electric mixer for 1–2 minutes, or until thick and smooth. Return to the container, freeze for 3 hours and repeat beating and freezing twice more before pouring into the container to freeze overnight.

3 To make the raspberry sauce, place the raspberries, sugar and lemon juice in a food processor, and process until smooth. Strain to remove the seeds.

4 Serve the sorbet on chilled plates with the sauce.

# Yule log

*The shape of this traditional French Christmas cake is inspired by the yule log that burns on the hearth on Christmas Eve. The yule log fire is said to represent the triumph of light over darkness.*

*Preparation time **45 minutes + refrigeration***
*Total cooking time **25 minutes***
*Serves **8–12***

### CHOCOLATE SPONGE CAKE
*2 eggs*
*1/4 cup sugar*
*1/3 cup all-purpose flour*
*1 tablespoon unsweetened cocoa*

### BUTTERCREAM
*1 oz. bittersweet chocolate, chopped*
*1/3 cup sugar*
*2 egg yolks*
*1 cup unsalted butter, softened*

### GANACHE
*8 oz. bittersweet chocolate, chopped*
*2/3 cup heavy cream*
*2 tablespoons unsalted butter*

*ready-made marzipan and coloring, to decorate*

1   To make the chocolate sponge cake, preheat the oven to 400°F. Line an 11 x 7 x 11/2-inches jelly roll pan with wax paper. Put the eggs and sugar in the top of a double boiler over barely steaming water, off the heat, making sure the insert does not touch the water. Using an electric mixer, beat for 5–7 minutes, or until the mixture is thick and creamy, has doubled in volume and leaves a trail as it falls from the beaters. The mixture should never be hot, only warm. Remove the insert from the water and beat until cold. Sift the flour and cocoa and carefully fold into the egg mixture until just combined. Pour into the prepared pan and spread evenly. Bake for

6–8 minutes, or until springy. Slide the hot sponge cake, with the paper, onto a wire rack.

2   To make the buttercream, put the chocolate in the top of a double boiler over hot water, off the heat, making sure the insert is not touching the water. Leave the chocolate to melt slowly, stirring occasionally until smooth. Cool slightly. Put the sugar in a small saucepan with enough cold water to just cover it. Make a sugar syrup by following the method in the Chef's techniques on page 62. Meanwhile, beat the egg yolks in a small bowl with an electric mixer until pale. As soon as the syrup is ready, carefully pour it in a thin steady stream into the egg yolks, beating constantly and pouring between the beaters and the side of the bowl. Continue beating until cold. Beat in the butter and then the melted chocolate. Place in a clean bowl and cover with plastic wrap.

3   To make the ganache, melt the chocolate as in step 2. Heat the cream until just at boiling point. Pour the cream into the chocolate and whisk until thick and glossy. Stir in the butter until melted, then cool to room temperature.

4   Turn the cake over onto a large piece of waxed paper and peel off the paper that was used for baking. Spread the ganache over the cake and roll it up by picking up the paper at one of the long sides and pushing it away from you while rolling. Trim the ends and chill for 5–10 minutes. Put the buttercream in a pastry bag fitted with a 1/2-inch star nozzle. Pipe lines of buttercream lengthwise along the log, then pipe swirls of buttercream on top. Alternatively, spread the butter cream with a palette knife. Chill, then use a fork to mark lines and notches for a bark effect.

5   Decorate the log with marzipan holly leaves and berries. Color the marzipan with food coloring, and cut out green leaves using a sharp knife and roll red berries between your fingers.

# Hot chocolate soufflés

*A well-risen, feather-light soufflé is one of the hallmarks of a great chef. The real difficulty lies in transporting the soufflé to the table before it begins to cool and collapses.*

Preparation time **20 minutes**
Total cooking time **20–25 minutes**
**Serves 6**

**2 oz. semisweet chocolate,
    coarsely chopped**
**1 cup milk**
**1/4 cup unsalted butter**
**1/4 cup all-purpose flour**
**sugar, to coat dishes**
**4 eggs, separated**
**3 tablespoons sugar**
**1 tablespoon unsweetened cocoa, sifted**
**confectioners' sugar, to dust**

1  Preheat the oven to 350°F. Put the chocolate in a bowl. Heat the milk in a saucepan until just at boiling point. Pour onto the chocolate and stir until the chocolate has melted. Melt the butter in a saucepan and add the flour. Cook over low heat for 1 minute. Add the chocolate milk gradually, stirring constantly with a wooden spoon. Bring to a boil and remove from the heat. Set aside to cool completely.

2  Brush six 4 x 2 inch, 1-cup soufflé dishes or custard cups with melted butter, working the brush from the bottom upwards. Refrigerate until the butter is firm, then repeat. Half fill one of the dishes with sugar and, without placing your fingers inside the mold, rotate so that a layer of sugar sticks to the butter. Tap out the excess sugar and use to coat the other molds. Discard the excess.

3  Stir the egg yolks into the chocolate mixture. In a separate bowl, beat the egg whites with an electric mixer until soft peaks form. Add the 3 tablespoons sugar and beat for 30 seconds. Fold in the cocoa. Lightly beat a third of the egg whites into the chocolate mixture to just blend. Add the rest of the egg whites and fold in very gently but quickly. Do not overmix or the mixture will lose its volume.

4  Spoon in the mixture to fill each dish completely and level the top with a palette knife. Sprinkle with sifted confectioners' sugar and then run your thumb just inside the top of the dish to create a ridge, which will enable the soufflé mixture to rise evenly. Bake for 15 minutes, or until the soufflés are well risen and a light crust has formed. The soufflés should feel just set when pressed lightly with your fingers. Dust the tops lightly with the sifted confectioners' sugar and serve the soufflés immediately.

# Chocolate rum truffles

*In the true style of truffles, these confections are highly decadent and very rich.*
*They are delicious served with coffee as a special after-dinner treat.*

*Preparation time **40 minutes + refrigeration***
*Total cooking time **10 minutes***
*Makes 24*

**10 oz. semisweet chocolate,**
  **finely chopped**
**1/3 cup heavy cream**
**1 teaspoon vanilla extract**
**2 tablespoons dark rum**
**unsweetened cocoa, to dust**

1 Put the chopped chocolate in a bowl. Place the cream and vanilla in a small saucepan and heat until it is just at boiling point. Pour the cream directly into the chopped chocolate. Gently mix with a whisk until the mixture is smooth. If there are any lumps, place the bowl over a saucepan of barely steaming water, off the heat, and stir lightly for a moment to melt any remaining chocolate. Mix in the rum and refrigerate the ganache until it is set.

2 Form the ganache into small balls using a melon baller, or pipe it into small balls using a pastry bag fitted with a plain nozzle. Return to the refrigerator to set. Roll the balls between your palms to form a perfect ball, then roll in the cocoa, using a fork to roll them around until evenly coated.

***Chef's tip*** Since these truffles are not dipped in chocolate before they are rolled in the cocoa powder, they should be eaten within 2–3 days. Store in an airtight container in the refrigerator. Roll the truffles in the cocoa powder a second time before serving.

# Chocolate roulade

*Whipped cream and fresh raspberries fill this delicate chocolate cake roll. It is
also delicious with other fresh fruits, such as strawberries or peaches.*

*Preparation time **25 minutes + 20 minutes refrigeration***
*Total cooking time **8–10 minutes***
***Serves 6***

**CHOCOLATE SPONGE CAKE**
**2 eggs**
**1/4 cup sugar**
**1/3 cup all-purpose flour**
**1 tablespoon unsweetened cocoa**

**FILLING**
**2/3 cup whipping cream**
**3 tablespoons confectioners' sugar**
**1 pint fresh raspberries**

**unsweetened cocoa and confectioners' sugar, to dust**

**1** To make the sponge cake, preheat the oven to 400°F. Line a 11 x 7 x 1 1/2-inches jelly roll pan with waxed paper. Put the eggs and sugar in the top of a double boiler over barely steaming water, off the heat, making sure the insert is not touching the water. Using an electric mixer, beat for 5–7 minutes, or until the mixture becomes thick and creamy, has doubled in volume and leaves a trail as it falls from the beaters. The temperature of the mixture should never be hot, only warm. Remove the insert from the water and continue to beat until the mixture is cold.

**2** Sift the flour and cocoa together and, using a large metal spoon, carefully fold it into the egg mixture. Stop folding as soon as the flour and cocoa are just combined or the mixture will lose its volume. Pour the mixture into the pan and spread it evenly using a palette knife. Bake for 6–8 minutes, or until springy to the light touch of a finger. Remove the cake from the pan while still hot by sliding it, with the paper on, to a wire rack to cool. Leave to cool, then turn it over onto a large piece of waxed paper or clean cloth and remove the paper that was used for baking.

**3** To make the filling, beat the cream with the confectioners' sugar until firm peaks form. Spread the cream onto the cake and sprinkle with the raspberries. Roll up by picking up the paper or cloth at one of the longer sides and pushing it down and away from you while rolling, finishing with the seam underneath. Trim each end and refrigerate for 20 minutes. Sprinkle sifted cocoa and confectioners' sugar onto the roulade.

# Warm chocolate puddings with pistachio cream

*These little chocolate puddings, served with a sweet pistachio cream and
poached pears, are an ideal winter dessert.*

*Preparation time **20 minutes***
*Total cooking time **35 minutes***
***Serves 8***

**PISTACHIO CREAM**
**3 tablespoons chopped pistachio nuts**
**I cup milk**
**3 egg yolks**
**3 tablespoons sugar**
**I–2 drops vanilla extract**

**6 oz. semisweet chocolate, chopped**
**1/3 cup unsalted butter, softened**
**1/4 cup unsweetened cocoa, sifted**
**6 eggs, separated**
**I cup sugar**
**poached or canned pears, drained and sliced, to serve**

1  To make the pistachio cream, toast the pistachios under a broiler for 1–2 minutes, shaking to make sure they don't burn. Grind the nuts to a paste using a mortar and pestle or a food processor. Pour the milk into a saucepan and heat slowly until just at boiling point.

Meanwhile, cream together the egg yolks and sugar until pale. Pour the milk into the yolks, mixing well. Transfer to a clean pan and cook gently over low heat, stirring constantly, until the mixture begins to thicken and coats the back of a spoon. Remove from the heat immediately, strain into a bowl and stir in the vanilla extract, to taste. Whisk in the pistachio paste and chill.

2  Preheat the oven to 325°F. Brush eight 3 x 11/2 inch, 1/2-cup soufflé dishes or custard cups with melted butter. Put the chocolate in the top of a double boiler over hot water, off the heat, and allow it to melt slowly, stirring occasionally. Cream the 1/3 cup butter until soft with a wooden spoon. Stir in the cocoa and fold the mixture into the chocolate.

3  In a separate bowl, beat the egg yolks and 1/2 cup of the sugar until doubled in volume, then fold into the chocolate mixture. Beat the egg whites until stiff peaks form. Add the remaining sugar and beat to a stiff, shiny meringue. Fold carefully into the chocolate mixture in three additions until just combined. Spoon into the dishes to three-quarters full. Bake for about 25 minutes, or until set, then remove from the dishes and place on individual plates. Pour the chilled pistachio cream around and serve immediately with the pears.

# Opéra

*Adapted from a complex French recipe, this dessert is a true work of art. It consists of layers of sponge cake, chocolate ganache, buttercream and coffee syrup, finished with a rich chocolate frosting.*

Preparation time **1 hour 45 minutes + refrigeration**
Total cooking time **1 hour**
Serves **4–6**

### ALMOND SPONGE CAKE
*2/3 cup confectioners' sugar*
*3 tablespoons all-purpose flour*
*2 1/2 oz. ground almonds*
*3 eggs*
*1 tablespoon unsalted butter, melted and cooled*
*3 egg whites*
*1 tablespoon sugar*

### CHOCOLATE GANACHE
*6 oz. semisweet chocolate, finely chopped*
*1/2 cup milk*
*1/2 cup heavy cream*
*3 tablespoons unsalted butter, softened*

### COFFEE SYRUP
*2 tablespoons sugar*
*2 tablespoons instant coffee*

### BUTTERCREAM
*1/3 cup sugar*
*1 egg white*
*1 tablespoon instant coffee*
*1/3 cup unsalted butter, softened*

**1** To make the sponge cake, preheat the oven to 425°F. Line an 11 x 7 x 1 1/2-inches jelly roll pan with waxed paper. Sift the confectioners' sugar and flour into a large bowl. Stir in the almonds. Add the eggs and beat until pale. Fold in the butter. Beat the egg whites until stiff, add the sugar and beat until stiff peaks form. Beat a third of the egg whites into the almond mixture, then carefully fold in the remainder until just combined. Pour onto the pan and gently spread. Bake for 6–7 minutes, or until golden and springy. Loosen the edges with the point of a knife. Turn out onto a wire rack covered with wax paper. Do not remove the paper used in baking.

**2** To make the ganache, put the chocolate in a bowl. Heat the milk and 2 tablespoons of the cream until just at boiling point. Pour into the chocolate, add the butter and whisk until smooth. Allow to set until spreadable.

**3** To make the coffee syrup, put the sugar and 1/3 cup water in a small saucepan and stir until dissolved. Bring to a boil and add the coffee.

**4** To make the buttercream, put the sugar and 1 tablespoon water in a small heavy-bottomed pan. Make a sugar syrup by following the method in the Chef's techniques on page 62. Meanwhile, beat the egg white until very soft peaks form. Continue beating and carefully pour in the hot syrup, pouring between the beaters and the side of the bowl. Beat until cold. Dissolve the coffee in 1 teaspoon of boiling water, cool to room temperature and add to the butter. Beat in half the egg white, then carefully fold in the other half until well combined.

**5** Cut the cake crosswise into three pieces. Soak one piece with a third of the coffee syrup, then spread with half the buttercream. Cover with the second piece of cake, soak with syrup and spread with half the ganache. Cover with the last piece of cake, soak with the remaining syrup and top with the remaining buttercream. Smooth the top and refrigerate until the buttercream is firmly set.

**6** Melt the remaining ganache in the top of a double boiler. Heat the remaining cream until just at boiling point and stir into the ganache. Cool until spreadable and spread over the top of the cake.

# Chocolate tart

*With a creamy chocolate center and pastry that melts in your mouth, this tart is delicious accompanied by a whiskey-flavored ice cream or a spoonful of vanilla-flavored Chantilly cream.*

*Preparation time **50 minutes***
   *+ **1 hour 40 minutes** refrigeration*
*Total cooking time **30–35 minutes***
***Serves 8***

**PASTRY**
**¹/2 cup unsalted butter, softened**
**3 tablespoons sugar**
**I egg, beaten**
**I–2 drops vanilla extract**
**I²/3 cups all-purpose flour, sifted**
**pinch of salt**

**8 oz. bittersweet chocolate, chopped**
**2 eggs**
**4 egg yolks**
**¹/4 cup sugar**
**³/4 cup softened unsalted butter, cut into cubes**
**confectioners' sugar, to dust**

**1** To make the pastry, cream the butter and sugar together with a wooden spoon. Gradually beat in the egg and the vanilla, beating well after each addition. (The mixture may look slightly curdled.) Add the flour and salt, and mix lightly until smooth. Do not overmix. Gather the pastry together into a rough ball. Flatten with the palm of your hand to a thickness of ¹/2 inch, wrap in plastic wrap and refrigerate for 20 minutes.

**2** Grease a 9¹/2 x 1-inch fluted tart pan with a removable base. Preheat the oven to 350°F.

**3** Roll the pastry out on a floured surface to a circle about 1/8-inch thick. Fold half the pastry over the rolling pin and lift it into the tart pan. Ease the sides of the pastry into the flutes or sides of the pan by using a small ball of lightly floured excess pastry held between your forefinger and thumb. Trim off any excess pastry with a sharp knife or roll over the top of the pan with a rolling pin. Chill for 20 minutes. Cut an 11-inch circle of waxed paper, crush it into a ball to soften the paper, then open and lay it inside the pastry shell so that it comes up the sides. Fill with pie weights or rice up to the rim, then press down gently, so the weights rest firmly against the sides of the shell. Bake for 10 minutes, or until firm. Remove the weights and paper. Return to the oven and continue to bake for 5–10 minutes, or until the center begins to color. Remove from the oven and set aside to cool.

**4** Put the chocolate in the top of a double boiler over hot water, off the heat, making sure the insert is not touching the water, and allow the chocolate to melt slowly, stirring occasionally. Transfer the chocolate to a large bowl and keep warm. Place the eggs, egg yolks and sugar in the cleaned top of the double boiler over barely steaming water and beat with an electric mixer until pale and four times its original volume.

**5** Stir one piece of butter at a time into the chocolate until melted. Gently fold in the egg mixture until thoroughly combined, but do not overmix or it will lose its volume. Pour into the pastry shell and bake for 10 minutes. Cool slightly before removing from the pan. Cool, then chill for 1 hour before serving. Dust with confectioners' sugar.

***Chef's tip*** Freeze any leftover pastry for later use.

# Orange-flavored chocolate-dipped cookies

*The word cookie originates from the Dutch koekje, which means little cakes. These "little cakes" are dipped in dark chocolate for an elegant touch.*

*Preparation time* **15 minutes + refrigeration**
*Total cooking time* **7–8 minutes**
*Makes 18*

**1/3 cup unsalted butter, at room temperature**
**3 tablespoons sugar**
**finely grated rind of 1/2 orange**
**1 cup self-rising flour (see Chef's tips)**
**3 oz. semisweet chocolate, chopped**

1  Preheat the oven to 375°F. Brush a baking sheet with melted butter. Soften the butter with a wooden spoon, gradually add the sugar and orange rind, and beat until light and pale. Sift the flour and stir it into the butter mixture until just combined. Roll the mixture into balls the size of a walnut. Place on the baking sheet and flatten with a wet fork. Bake for 7–8 minutes, or until golden brown. Cool on a wire rack.

2  Meanwhile, put the chocolate in the top of a double boiler over hot water, off the heat, making sure the insert is not touching the water, and allow to melt slowly, stirring until smooth. Dip one side of each cookie into the chocolate and lay on waxed paper. Refrigerate the cookies until the chocolate is just set.

*Chef's tips* If self-rising flour is not available, substitute with 1 cup all-purpose flour sifted with 3/4 teaspoon baking powder.

These cookies may be stored in an airtight container for up to a week.

# Irish coffee cream

*If you simply can't wait for the ganache to go cold before you indulge in this treat, try serving it warm.*

*Preparation time* **10 minutes + refrigeration**
*Total cooking time* **3–5 minutes**
*Serves 4*

**GANACHE**
**6 oz. bittersweet chocolate, chopped**
**3/4 cup heavy cream**
**2 1/2 tablespoons sugar**
**1 tablespoon whiskey**

**COFFEE CREAM**
**3/4 cup whipping cream**
**1/4 cup confectioners' sugar, sifted**
**1 tablespoon instant coffee dissolved in 1 teaspoon hot water**

**unsweetened cocoa, to dust**

1  To make the ganache, put the chocolate in a bowl. Put the cream and sugar in a saucepan and heat until just at boiling point. Pour directly into the chocolate and whisk or stir well until smooth and creamy. (If the chocolate does not melt, stir over a pan of hot water, making sure the bowl is not touching the water.) Mix in the whiskey. Refrigerate to cool, mixing from time to time to prevent a crust from forming on the surface.

2  Divide the ganache among four glasses or goblets, and chill while preparing the coffee cream.

3  To make the coffee cream, beat the cream and sugar until firm peaks form. Mix in the dissolved coffee. Pipe the coffee cream onto the ganache, then lightly dust with cocoa before serving.

*Orange-flavored chocolate-dipped cookies (bottom) and Irish coffee cream*

# Chocolate beignets

*These little fritters are crisp on the outside, with a soft, chocolaty filling.*
*They are delicious served hot with vanilla ice cream.*

*Preparation time* **1 hour 20 minutes + chilling**
*Total cooking time* **30 minutes**
**Makes 48**

**10 oz. semisweet chocolate, chopped**
**3/4 cup heavy cream**
**unsweetened cocoa, to dust**
**oil, for deep-frying**
**flour, to dust**

**BEIGNET BATTER**
**2 cups all-purpose flour**
**4 teaspoons cornstarch**
**1 tablespoon oil**
**pinch of salt**
**1 egg**
**1 cup beer (preferably a light lager)**
**2 egg whites**
**1 tablespoon sugar**

**1** Put the chopped chocolate in the top of a double boiler over hot water, off the heat, making sure the insert is not touching the water, and allow to melt slowly, stirring occasionally. Remove the insert from the water. Heat the cream in a small saucepan until it is just boiling. Pour into the chocolate and whisk until smooth. Scrape the sides of the bowl, cover and chill until set.

**2** Once the chocolate has set, scoop it into a pastry bag and pipe out 48 small balls onto waxed paper—don't worry if they are not perfectly round. Refrigerate until hardened, then roll them between your hands to form uniform balls, using unsweetened cocoa to prevent them from sticking too much. Freeze until solid.

**3** To make the batter, mix the flour and cornstarch together in a large bowl, and make a well in the center. Add the oil, salt and egg, and mix together, gradually incorporating the flour. Once a smooth paste has formed, mix in the beer, a little at a time. Continue working until the batter is smooth.

**4** Take a deep-fat fryer or large heavy-bottomed saucepan and fill one-third full with oil and preheat to 375°F. Beat the egg whites until firm, then beat in the sugar and gently fold the egg whites into the batter.

**5** Remove two or three chocolate balls at a time from the freezer and lightly coat them with some flour. Using tongs, dip the balls into the batter and place directly into the hot oil. Fry for 3–5 minutes, or until lightly browned. Do not fry too many at once or the oil temperature will drop. Remove immediately and drain on paper towels. Continue with the remaining balls. Lightly dust with cocoa and serve immediately.

***Chef's tip*** Make sure the chocolate is completely frozen before deep-frying. If you can, prepare the chocolate balls the day before and freeze them overnight.

# Creamy chocolate soufflés

*This soufflé has a creamier texture than a conventional soufflé, so it won't*
*rise as much. It is best baked in individual shallow dishes.*

*Preparation time **10 minutes***
*Total cooking time **15 minutes***
*Serves 4*

**3 oz. semisweet chocolate, chopped**
**1/4 cup unsalted butter**
**1/4 cup unsweetened cocoa**
**2 eggs, separated**
**sugar, to coat dishes**
**2 egg whites**
**1/3 cup confectioners' sugar, sifted,**
**plus extra to dust**
**vanilla ice cream or orange sorbet, to serve**

1  Preheat the oven to 400°F. Put the chocolate in the top of a double boiler over hot water, off the heat, making sure the insert is not touching the water, and allow to melt slowly, stirring occasionally. Add the butter and whisk until smooth. Sift the cocoa into the chocolate and mix well. Remove the insert from the water. Whisk the egg yolks, then add them to the chocolate mixture.

2  Lightly butter four 5 x 1 inch, 11/4-cup gratin dishes or ramekins. Coat lightly with some of the sugar and set aside. Beat the egg whites in a large bowl until stiff peaks form. Gradually beat in the confectioners' sugar and beat until the whites are firm and shiny. Gently fold a third of the egg whites into the chocolate mixture. Once incorporated, fold in the remaining egg whites.

3  Divide the mixture among the dishes. Sprinkle with confectioners' sugar and bake for about 8 minutes, or until the soufflés are just set to the light touch of a finger. Place a scoop of vanilla ice cream or orange sorbet in the center of the soufflés and serve immediately.

***Chef's tip*** Eggs are easiest to separate when they are cold, straight from the refrigerator. However, to get maximum volume from egg whites, they are best beaten at room temperature. Egg whites should be beaten in a clean dry bowl with clean, dry beaters. Any hint of grease will prevent them from stiffening.

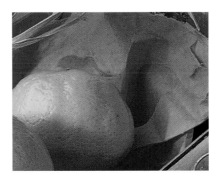

# Chocolate-dipped fruits

*Surely this is the way fruit was intended to be . . . sweet and juicy, and smothered with rich dark chocolate. The combination of fruits you use is only limited by your imagination.*

*Preparation time* **20 minutes + 15 minutes refrigeration**
*Total cooking time* **10–15 minutes**
**Serves 4–6**

**3¹/₃ cups strawberries**
**2 clementines or tangerines**
**6 oz. bittersweet chocolate, chopped**
**1 tablespoon oil**

**1** Line a baking sheet with wax paper. Clean the strawberries by brushing with a dry pastry brush, or rinsing them very quickly in cold water and drying well on a thick layer of paper towels. Discard any berries with soft spots. Peel the clementines or tangerines and remove as much of the white pith as possible, then break the fruit into individual segments.

**2** Put the chocolate in the top of a double boiler over hot water, off the heat, making sure the insert is not touching the water. Leave the chocolate to melt, stirring occasionally. Stir in the oil, and mix until completely incorporated. Remove the pan from the water and place on a folded towel to keep it warm.

**3** Holding the berries by their stems or hulls, dip each about three quarters of the way into the chocolate, so that some of the color of the fruit still shows. Gently wipe off any excess chocolate on the edge of the bowl and place the coated strawberries on their sides on the baking sheet. Repeat with the clementines or tangerines, drying each segment on paper towels before dipping. If the chocolate becomes too thick, reheat the water, remove from the heat and replace the insert until the chocolate returns to the required consistency.

**4** Once all the fruit has been dipped in the chocolate, place in the refrigerator for 15 minutes, or until the chocolate has just set. Remove from the refrigerator and keep in a cool place until ready to serve. Do not serve directly from the refrigerator—the cold temperature will inhibit the full flavor and sweetness of the fruit, and the chocolate will be too hard.

***Chef's tips*** Any fruit can be used, but the best results are with ones that can be left whole or have a dry surface.

If the strawberry stems are too short, use a toothpick to dip them.

Use a small pair of tongs for the citrus fruit slices—do not use a toothpick as it will pierce the fruit, and the juices will stop the chocolate from coating evenly.

# Truffle torte

*This is a truly decadent, rich chocolate dessert. Serve it just as it is with a strong espresso or with a bowl of fresh raspberries. Either way, this smooth, rich torte is enough to impress anyone.*

Preparation time **1 hour 30 minutes + refrigeration**
Total cooking time **20 minutes**
**Serves 8**

**CHOCOLATE SPONGE CAKE**
**2 eggs**
**3 tablespoons sugar**
**1/3 cup all-purpose flour**
**I tablespoon unsweetened cocoa**

**2 tablespoons rum**
**I lb. semisweet chocolate,**
  **chopped**
**I teaspoon gelatin powder**
**1/4 cup light corn syrup**
**2 cups whipping cream**
**unsweetened cocoa, to dust**

**1** To make the sponge cake, preheat the oven to 325°F. Butter and flour an 8 x 2 1/4-inch round springform pan. Put the eggs and sugar in the top of a double boiler over hot water, off the heat, making sure the insert is not touching the water. Using an electric mixer, beat for 5–10 minutes, or until the mixture is thick and light, has doubled in volume and leaves a trail as it falls from the beaters. The temperature of the mixture should never be hot, only warm. Remove the insert from the water and continue to beat until cold.

**2** Sift the flour and cocoa together and carefully fold into the egg mixture with a large metal spoon or plastic spatula, until just combined. Pour the mixture into the baking pan, gently smooth the top with the back of a spoon and bake for about 15 minutes, or until springy

and shrinking from the side of the pan. Turn the sponge cake out onto a wire rack to cool. Clean the springform to use again later.

**3** Trim the top crust off the cake using a long serrated knife. Cut the cake into a layer no more than 5/8-inch thick to just fit inside the springform and place directly on the bottom of the pan. Using a pastry brush, brush the cake layer with rum.

**4** Put 10 oz. of the chocolate in the top of a double boiler over hot water, off the heat, and allow to melt slowly, stirring until smooth. Remove the insert from the water. Stir the gelatin powder and 1 tablespoon water over a pan of simmering water until dissolved. Pour 1/3 cup water into a small saucepan, add the corn syrup and bring to a boil. Remove from the heat. Stir the dissolved gelatin powder into the warm corn syrup until completely combined. Pour into the chocolate, mixing thoroughly with a small wire whisk. If this mixture is lumpy, heat very gently over a pan of barely steaming water off the heat until smooth. Cool.

**5** Beat the cream until soft peaks form, and fold it into the cooled chocolate mixture. Do not overmix. Fill the springform to the top with the truffle mixture and level with a palette knife. Chill for several hours, or until set.

**6** Hold a hot, damp towel around the springform for 30 seconds and lift out the torte. Dust the torte with the cocoa and mark it with the back of a knife in a trellis fashion. Melt the remaining chocolate in a double boiler over hot water as before. Pour onto a sheet of nonstick waxed paper and spread to a thickness of 1/8 inch with a large palette knife. Refrigerate until set. Break off large pieces of chocolate from the paper and stick onto the side of the torte. Transfer the torte, on the springform base, to a large plate to serve.

# Petits pots au chocolat

*These dainty little chocolate custards are prepared and cooked in a very similar way to crème caramel, except that they are much richer, with a fine, smooth texture that melts in the mouth.*

*Preparation time **10 minutes + refrigeration***
*Total cooking time **45 minutes***
***Serves 6***

**1 1/2 cups milk**
**1/3 cup whipping cream**
**2 oz. semisweet chocolate, chopped**
**1/2 vanilla bean, split lengthwise**
**1 egg**
**3 egg yolks**
**1/3 cup sugar**
**whipped cream and grated chocolate,**
  **to serve**

1 Preheat the oven to 325°F. Place the milk, cream, chocolate and vanilla bean in a heavy-bottomed saucepan and bring to a boil. Using a wooden spoon, cream the egg, egg yolks and sugar together until thick and light. Pour in the melted chocolate mixture and stir to blend. Strain into a large liquid measuring cup and discard the vanilla bean. Remove any froth by skimming across the top with a metal spoon.

2 Pour the mixture into six 1/3-cup ceramic pots or espresso cups, filling them up to the top. Set the pots in a baking dish and pour in enough hot water to come up to about 1/2 inch below their rims. Bake for 30 minutes, or until the surface of the custard feels elastic when you touch it with your finger, and your finger comes away clean. If this is not the case, continue to cook for a little while longer.

3 Remove the pots from the water bath and allow to cool. Once the pots are cold, place the whipped cream in a pastry bag fitted with a star-shaped nozzle. Pipe rosettes of cream onto the top of the pots and sprinkle with a little grated chocolate to serve.

# Symphony of three chocolates

*The harmonious composition of the layers of creamy white, milk and dark chocolate mousse*
*will be sweet music to your mouth.*

*Preparation time **1 hour + 3 hours refrigeration***
*Total cooking time **20 minutes***
***Serves 8–10***

### ITALIAN MERINGUE
*3/4 cup sugar*
*6 egg whites*

### WHITE CHOCOLATE MOUSSE
*1/2 teaspoon gelatin powder*
*2 oz. white chocolate, chopped*
*2 tablespoons Cointreau*
*1/4 cup whipping cream, whipped*
*juice of 1/4 lemon*

### MILK CHOCOLATE MOUSSE
*1/2 teaspoon gelatin powder*
*2 oz. milk chocolate, chopped*
*1/4 cup whipping cream, whipped*

### SEMISWEET CHOCOLATE MOUSSE
*1/2 teaspoon gelatin powder*
*2 oz. semisweet chocolate, chopped*
*1/4 cup whipping cream, whipped*

1  To make the Italian meringue, put the sugar and 1/4 cup water in a small saucepan. Make a sugar syrup by following the method in the Chef's techniques on page 62. Meanwhile, beat the egg whites with an electric mixer until stiff peaks form. When the syrup is ready, immediately dip the bottom of the pan in cold water to stop the cooking process. Carefully pour the hot syrup into the egg whites in a steady stream, beating constantly and pouring between the beaters and the side of the bowl. Continue beating at moderate speed until the mixture is completely cool. Cover with plastic wrap.

2  Lightly grease a 91/4 x 3 x 21/2-inch, 1-quart terrine or mold and line the bottom with waxed paper extending over the sides of the dish.

3  To make the white chocolate mousse, stir the gelatin powder and 1 tablespoon water over a pan of simmering water until dissolved. Put the white chocolate in the top of a double boiler over hot water, off the heat, and allow to melt slowly, stirring until smooth. Place the dissolved gelatin powder in a small saucepan with the Cointreau and warm over very low heat. Fold a third of the whipped cream into the melted chocolate. Mix some of this into the gelatin mixture, then fold the gelatin into the chocolate mixture. Fold in the remaining cream, a third of the Italian meringue and the lemon juice. Transfer to the terrine and spread in an even layer using the back of a spoon. Refrigerate to set.

4  To make the milk chocolate mousse, follow the same method as step 3, replacing the Cointreau with 2 tablespoons water and omitting the lemon juice. Spread evenly over the white chocolate mousse and return to the refrigerator until set.

5  To make the semisweet chocolate mousse, follow the same method as step 3, replacing the Cointreau with 2 tablespoons water and omitting the lemon juice. Spread evenly over the milk chocolate mousse. Refrigerate for at least 3 hours, or overnight.

6  To unmold the mousse, run the tip of a knife along the edge of the terrine or mold. Dip the bottom in hot water for a few seconds, place a cutting board on top and flip over. Hold the terrine and cutting board securely and shake downwards. Repeat this process if necessary. Gently lift the terrine away. Cut into slices to serve.

# White chocolate fudge

*Made with creamy white chocolate, this fudge is
ultra sweet, so eat it in small quantities, if you can.*

*Preparation time **15 minutes** + **2 hours refrigeration***
*Total cooking time **7 minutes***
***Makes about 50 pieces***

**1 1/3 cups sugar**
**2 tablespoons unsalted butter**
**pinch of salt**
**1/2 cup evaporated milk**
**1 vanilla bean**
**10 oz. white chocolate, chopped**
**1/2 cup shelled, peeled pistachio nuts**

**1** Grease a 7 or 8-inch square cake pan. Put the sugar,
butter, salt and evaporated milk in a large saucepan.
Split the vanilla bean in half lengthwise and scrape
the small black seeds into the saucepan with the point
of a knife. Add the bean to the saucepan. Bring to a boil
over medium heat, stirring constantly with a wooden
spoon. Lower the heat and simmer for about 5 minutes,
stirring constantly.

**2** Remove the saucepan from the heat and lift out the
vanilla bean with a fork or slotted spoon. Stir in the
chopped chocolate until it has melted completely and
the mixture is smooth. Stir in the pistachios and pour
into the pan. Refrigerate for about 2 hours, or until firm.

**3** Cut into small squares and serve in paper
confectionery wrappers. The fudge can be stored in the
refrigerator for up to a week.

**Chef's tips** Chopped hazelnuts (filberts) may be
substituted for the pistachios.

Using a vanilla bean will give a delicious flavor to the
fudge, but if you wish to avoid seeing the black seeds,
use 1/2 teaspoon vanilla extract instead.

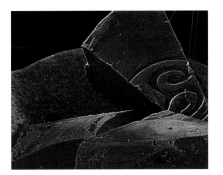

# Chocolate génoise

*This recipe is named after the city of Genoa, where this classic sponge cake is thought to have been created. The secret to a successful génoise sponge cake is in treating the mixture carefully. If the eggs and sugar are beaten correctly, and the flour is lightly folded through, the result should be feather-light.*

Preparation time **15 minutes + cooling**
Total cooking time **35–40 minutes**
**Serves 8–10**

**4 eggs**
**1/3 cup sugar**
**2/3 cup all-purpose flour**
**2 1/2 tablespoons unsweetened cocoa**
**4 teaspoons unsalted butter, melted**
**1/2 cup raspberry jam**
**confectioners' sugar, to dust**

1 Preheat the oven to 350°F. Grease and lightly flour an 8-inch springform pan. Put the eggs and sugar in the top of a double boiler over barely steaming water, off the heat, making sure the insert does not touch the water. Using an electric mixer, beat for 5–10 minutes, or until the mixture is thick and creamy, has doubled in volume and leaves a trail as it falls from the beaters. The mixture should never be hot, only warm. Remove the insert from the water and continue to beat until cold.

2 Sift the flour and cocoa together and, using a large metal spoon, carefully fold the mixture into the beaten eggs. Stop folding as soon as the dry ingredients are just combined or the mixture will lose its volume. Gently, but quickly, fold in the warm butter. Pour into the pan and bake on the middle rack of the oven for 25–30 minutes, or until springy to the light touch of a finger and shrinking from the sides of the pan. Turn out onto a wire rack, put another rack on top, turn over so the crust is upright, remove the rack that is now on top and leave to cool. This ensures that the top crust is not broken or marked by the wire.

3 Using a long serrated knife, cut the cold cake in half horizontally, cutting from one side to the other with a firm sawing action. Spread the bottom half with the raspberry jam. Place the other half on top, sprinkle with confectioners' sugar and carefully lift onto a plate.

***Chef's tips*** The saucepan of water in step 1 must not be too hot as this would cause the mixture to lose volume and the cake to be flat and heavy once cooked.

The unfilled cake may be frozen for 3 months.

# Chocolate mousse

*This sophisticated chocolate mousse is so light and creamy that it melts in the mouth. Try serving the mousse in chocolate cups, or layering with banana and rum, or amaretti cookies and whiskey.*

Preparation time **1 hour + 1 hour refrigeration**
Total cooking time **15 minutes**
***Serves 6***

**4 oz. semisweet chocolate**
**4 tablespoons sugar**
**2 egg whites**
**3/4 teaspoon gelatin powder**
**1 tablespoon instant coffee**
**2 cups whipping cream**

1  Grate enough of the chocolate to measure 2 tablespoons and set aside in a cool dry place. Put 1/4 cup water with the sugar in a small heavy-bottomed saucepan. Make a sugar syrup by following the method in the Chef's techniques on page 62. When the sugar starts to boil, beat the egg whites in a bowl using an electric mixer until they barely hold their shape in very soft peaks. With the machine still running, pour the bubbling syrup into the whites, aiming between the bowl and the beaters. Continue to beat until cold.

2  Stir the gelatin powder and 1 tablespoon water over a pan of simmering water until dissolved. Dissolve the instant coffee in 1 tablespoon of boiling water in a small saucepan, add the dissolved gelatin powder and warm over gentle heat. Do not boil or the gelatin will be stringy. Pour into the egg whites and stir well.

3  Coarsely chop the remaining chocolate and put in the top of a double boiler over hot water, off the heat, and allow to melt slowly, stirring until smooth. Remove the insert from the water and fold the chocolate into the egg white mixture.

4  Whip the cream until it leaves a trail when lifted on the whisk, then fold into the chocolate mixture. Stir in the grated chocolate. Pipe the mousse into six elegant glasses using a pastry bag fitted with a 5/8-inch plain nozzle. Refrigerate for 1 hour, or until the mousse has set.

5  As a final touch, the mousse can be decorated with small rosettes of whipped cream, or for a really elegant touch try addding some handmade chocolate leaves, grated chocolate or chocolate curls to serve (see Chef's techniques, page 63).

# Cointreau chocolate truffles

*These divine milk chocolate confections are flavored with a touch of Cointreau.*
*Rolled in confectioners' sugar, they're the perfect size to just pop in your mouth.*

*Preparation time **1 hour + refrigeration***
*Total cooking time **15 minutes***
***Makes 40***

❀ ❀ ❀

**1 1/4 lb. milk chocolate, chopped**
**1 oz. chocolate hazelnut spread**
**2 tablespoons Cointreau**
**4 teaspoons unsalted butter**
**1 1/2 cups confectioners' sugar**

**1** Line a baking sheet with wax paper. Put 8 oz. of the chocolate in the top of a double boiler over hot water, off the heat, making sure the insert is not touching the water, and allow the chocolate to melt slowly, stirring occasionally, until smooth. Remove the insert from the water.

**2** Place 2 tablespoons water with the hazelnut spread and Cointreau in a small saucepan, and bring to a boil. Pour into the melted chocolate and beat well with a wooden spoon. Stir in the butter, allow to cool, then refrigerate until the mixture is set. It should be stiff enough to hold its own shape when piped.

**3** Spoon the mixture into a pastry bag fitted with a 1/2-inch star-shaped nozzle, and pipe in long, straight, even lines onto the paper-lined baking sheet. Place in the refrigerator so the chocolate becomes firm.

**4** Meanwhile, temper the remaining chocolate by following the method in the Chef's techniques on page 62. Place the tempered chocolate over a bowl of lukewarm water to prevent it from setting.

**5** Cut the strips of piped chocolate into 1-inch lengths to fit into paper confectionery wrappers. Put the confectioners' sugar in a bowl. Using a fork, dip each truffle into the chocolate, one at a time, and shake off the excess by tapping the fork on the side of the bowl. Drop into the sugar and shake gently to coat. Allow to set in the sugar for a few minutes. Remove each truffle, shaking off any excess sugar, and place in paper wrappers. Store in an airtight container at room temperature until ready to use for after dinner treats with coffee.

# Chocolate sauce

*This is the ultimate topping for ice cream, but you'll find an excuse to serve it on almost anything.*

Preparation time **10 minutes**
Total cooking time **15 minutes**
**Serves 4–6**

**1 cup sugar**
**4 oz. semisweet chocolate, chopped**
**2 tablespoons unsweetened cocoa, sifted**

1 Put 1 1/4 cups water with the sugar and chocolate in a saucepan. Bring to a boil slowly, stirring constantly to dissolve the sugar and melt the chocolate, then remove from the heat.
2 Mix the cocoa with 2 tablespoons warm water to make a smooth paste. Spoon into the saucepan, stir and return to medium heat. Bring back to a boil, whisking vigorously. Simmer, uncovered, for 5 minutes without allowing the sauce to boil. Strain through a fine sieve and leave to cool a little.

**Chef's tip** This sauce may be served hot or cold and keeps well for up to 1 week if stored in an airtight container in the refrigerator.

# Hot chocolate drink

*If you've only ever experienced hot chocolate made with hot milk and cocoa, you'll die for this chocolate drink made with melted chocolate, milk and cream.*

Preparation time **10 minutes**
Total cooking time **15 minutes**
**Makes about 6 cups**

**1 quart milk**
**1 cup heavy cream**
**4 oz. semisweet chocolate, roughly chopped**
**1 teaspoon ground cinnamon**
**1 black peppercorn**
**1/4 cup sugar**

1 Pour the milk and cream into a saucepan and slowly bring to a boil over low heat. Add the chocolate, cinnamon, peppercorn and sugar, and gently simmer for at least 10 minutes.
2 The chocolate may be strained and served immediately, but the flavor will improve if it is refrigerated for a few hours or up to 3 days. Reheat to serve.

*Chocolate sauce (bottom) and Hot chocolate drink*

# Chef's techniques

◆

## Tempering chocolate

*Tempering chocolate breaks down the fat,
resulting in a hard, glossy chocolate.*

Place the chopped chocolate in a heatproof bowl and sit it over a pan of water that has just boiled. Leave the chocolate to melt slowly off the heat. The bowl must not touch the water at any time.

Stir the chocolate until it is smooth and reaches a temperature of 115°F.

Sit the bowl of melted chocolate in a large bowl filled with ice cubes. Stir until the temperature drops to 80°F.

Heat the chocolate again over the pan of hot water for 30–60 seconds, or until it reaches 89°F for semisweet chocolate; about 85°F for milk or white chocolate.

## Making a sugar syrup

*Wait until the sugar has completely dissolved before
boiling the liquid, and never stir once the syrup boils.*

Stir the sugar and water over low heat until the sugar dissolves completely.

Using a wet pastry brush, brush the sugar crystals from the side of the pan.

Boil, without stirring, until the syrup reaches the soft-ball stage, which is between 234°F and 240°F.

If you don't have a sugar thermometer, drop about 1/4 teaspoon of the syrup into a bowl of iced water. The syrup should form a soft ball that flattens when removed from the water.

# Making chocolate cups

*Ice cream, sorbet and mousse all look lovely served in elegant chocolate cups.*

Line the inside of brioche or other molds with plastic wrap, then fill with water. Place the molds in the freezer until frozen solid.

Melt the chocolate. Remove the ice from the molds, grasping the plastic wrap at the top, and immediately dip the plastic-covered ice mold into the melted chocolate.

Lift the ice mold from the chocolate and allow the excess to drain away. The chocolate should set immediately. Carefully peel away the plastic and discard the ice.

# Making chocolate leaves

*Use unsprayed leaves and make sure you wipe them with a damp towel, then allow to dry.*

Using a fine brush, paint one side of rose, ivy or other non-toxic shiny leaves with melted chocolate. The underside will give a more defined result.

Allow the chocolate to set, then carefully peel away the leaf from the chocolate.

# Making chocolate curls

*These curls can be sprinkled over almost any chocolate dish for a delicate finishing touch.*

Using a block of chocolate at room temperature, draw a vegetable peeler across the block. Vary the length of the scrapes to make shorter or longer curls.

First published in the United States in 1998 by Periplus Editions (HK) Ltd.

Murdoch Books and Le Cordon Bleu thank the 32 masterchefs of all the Le Cordon Bleu Schools, whose knowledge and expertise have made this book possible, especially: Chef Cliche (MOF), Chef Terrien, Chef Boucheret, Chef Duchêne (MOF), Chef Guillut, Chef Steneck, Paris; Chef Males, Chef Walsh, Chef Hardy, London; Chef Chantefort, Chef Bertin, Chef Jambert, Chef Honda, Tokyo; Chef Salembien, Chef Boutin, Chef Harris, Sydney; Chef Lawes, Adelaide; Chef Guiet, Chef Denis, Ottawa. Of the many students who helped the Chefs test each recipe, a special mention to graduates David Welch and Allen Wertheim. A very special acknowledgment to Directors Susan Eckstein, Great Britain, and Kathy Shaw, Paris, who have been responsible for the coordination of the Le Cordon Bleu team throughout this series.

The Publisher and Le Cordon Bleu also wish to thank Carole Sweetnam for her help with this series

First published in Australia in 1998 by Murdoch Books®

Managing Editor: Kay`Halsey
Series Concept, Design and Art Direction: Juliet Cohen
Editor: Justine Upex
Food Director: Jody Vassallo
Food Editors: Dimitra Stais, Kathy Knudsen, Tracy Rutherford
US Editor: Linda Venturoni Wilson
Designer: Norman Baptista
Photographer: Chris Jones
Food Stylist: Mary Harris
Food Preparation: Christine Sheppard, Kerrie Ray
Chef's Techniques Photographer: Reg Morrison
Home Economists: Michelle Lawton, Kerrie Mullins, Kerrie Ray

Library of Congress catalog card number: 98-65972
ISBN 962-593-431-6

Front cover: Truffle torte

Distributed in the United States by
Tuttle Publishing
Distribution Center
Airport Industrial Park
364 Innovation Drive
North Clarendon, VT 05759-9436
Tel: (802) 773-8930
Fax: (802) 773-6993

Printed in Singapore

05 04 03 02 01 00    10 9 8 7 6 5 4 3

Important: Some of the recipes in this book may include raw eggs, which can cause salmonella poisoning. Those who might be at risk from this (the elderly, pregnant women, young children and those suffering from immune deficiency diseases) should check with their physicians before eating raw eggs.